SOLO B♭ CLARINET

SWING WITH A B

To access audio visit:
www.halleonard.com/mylibrary

Enter Code
2694-6804-4133-0545

ISBN 978-1-59615-801-6

Visit Hal Leonard Online at
www.halleonard.com

Contact us:
Hal Leonard
7777 West Bluemound Road
Milwaukee, WI 53213
Email: info@halleonard.com

In Europe, contact:
Hal Leonard Europe Limited
42 Wigmore Street
Marylebone, London, W1U 2RN
Email: info@halleonardeurope.com

In Australia, contact:
Hal Leonard Australia Pty. Ltd.
4 Lentara Court
Cheltenham, Victoria, 3192 Australia
Email: info@halleonard.com.au

CONTENTS

B♭ CLARINET

DON'T BE THAT WAY

Brightly

Benny Goodman, Mitchell Parish
and Edgar Sampson

F
Dm
Gm7
C7(♯5)
Gm
(D.S. only)
CLAR. SOLO
E7
A♯°
A7
D7
G♯°
G7

F
Dm
Gm7
C7(♯5)
F
Dm
Gm7
C7(♯5)
F
Dm
Gm7
C7(♯5)
F
Gm7
C7(♯5)
F
Dm
Gm7
C7(♯5)
F
Dm
Gm7
C7(♯5)
F
Dm
Gm7
C7(♯5)
F
Gm7
G♯°
F
E7
A♯°
E7
A7
D7
G♯°
D7
G7
C7(♯5)
D.S. al CODA
CODA
5

B♭ CLARINET

I UNDERSTAND

Slowly, with feeling

Kim Gannon and Mabel Wayne

B♭ CLARINET

HOW AM I TO KNOW?

Dorthy Parker and Jack King

Moderately

CLARINET SOLO - (MELODY)

1 4 D9 Fm

9 Dm7 G7 C

13 D9 Fm

17 Dm7 G7 C Gm6

𝄋 21 A7 A7(♯5) A7 Fm6

25 Dm7 G7 C Cm6

29 D9 Fm

33 Dm7 G7 𝄌 C Fm6 C

CLAR. SOLO
D 9
F m
D m7
G 7
C
D 9
F m
D m7
G 7
C
G m6
A 7
A 7(♯5)
A 7
F m6
D m7
G 7
C
C m6
D 9
F m
D m7
G 7
C
F m6
C
D 9
F m
D m7
G 7
C
D 9
F m
D m7
G 7
C
G m6
D.S. al CODA
CODA
C
2

B♭ CLARINET

I GOT IT BAD
(And That Ain't Good)

Slowly, with feeling

Paul Francis Webster
and Duke Ellington

CLAR. SOLO
A° A C♯7 F♯m B9 F♯m B9
Bm7 C♯7(♯5) F♯9 B7 E7(♭9) A F♯m Bm B♭7(♭5)
A° A C♯7 F♯m B9 F♯m B9
Bm7 C♯7(♯5) F♯9 B7 E7(♭9) A Dm6 F♯° A7
D Dm6
G♯7 A C♯m7 F♯7 F♯7(♭9) Bm F7(♯5) E7
A° A C♯7 F♯m B9 F♯m B9
Bm7 C♯7(♯5) F♯9 B7 E7(♭9) A
3

I'LL NEVER BE THE SAME

B♭ CLARINET

Slowly, with feeling

Gus Kahn, Matt Malneck
and Frank Signorelli

Em7 A7 D7 Am7 D° D7 E♭7 D7
E♭7 D7 G Am7 B♭° G
G7 Dm7 G7 G7(♯5) C Dm7 D♯° C
Am Cm6 Dm6
E7 E♭7 D7 E♭7 D7 G G♯° Am7 D7
E♭7 D7 E♭7 D7 G Am7 B♭° G
G7 Dm7 G7 G7(♯5) C Dm7 D♯° C
Am Cm6 Dm6 E7
E♭7 D7 E♭7 D7 G
3

B♭ CLARINET

I'M IN THE MOOD FOR LOVE

Jimmy McHugh
and Dorothy Fields

CLAR. SOLO
D
Em7
A7
D
F♯m7
F°
Em7
A7
Dm
Em7
A7
D
Em7
A7
D
F♯m7
F°
Em7
A7
D
Em7
A7
D
Am6
B7
Gm6
A7
D
Bm6
C♯7
F♯m
Dm6
E7
Gm6
A7
D.S. al CODA
CODA
Em7
A7
D
(loco)

B♭ CLARINET

I'M THROUGH WITH LOVE

Gus Kahn, Matt Malneck
and Bud Livingston

Moderately, with feeling

CLARINET SOLO - (MELODY)

GMaj7 B♭° Am D7 Am7 GMaj9 G7(♯5) C Cm6
29
G Dm6 E7 Am Am7 D7 G
33
CLAR. SOLO
Bm G Bm6 G Bm G Bm6 E7
37
D D+ G6 A7 D Am7 D D7
41
3
3
GMaj7 B♭° Am D7 Am7 GMaj9 G7(♯5) C Cm6
45
G Dm6 E7 Am Am7 D7
49
G F9 B♭9 E♭9 Am7 A♭Maj7 G
52
3
3

CLARINET

ONE O'CLOCK JUMP

Brightly

Count Basie

ONE O'CLOCK JUMP
Count Basie

71
A♭9
E♭
B♭7
76
E♭
BASS SOLO
11
(ENS. LEAD)
91
96
TRPT. SOLO
101
E♭
E♭7
A♭9
108
E♭
F m7
E♭
115
E♭
E♭7
A♭9
121
E♭
F m7
125
1.
E♭
2.
E♭
E°
F m7
B♭7
E♭

B♭ CLARINET

STOMPIN' AT THE SAVOY

Brightly

Benny Goodman, Chick Webb
and Edgar Sampson

CLAR. SOLO
37 G D9 G G♯°
41 Am7 D7 D9 G D7
45 G D9 G G♯°
49 Am7 D7 D9 G
53 C7 D♭7 C7 F7 E♭m6 F7
57 B♭7 B7 B♭7 E♭7 D7 D9
61 G D9 G G♯°
65 Am7 D7 D9 G
69 G D9 G G♯° Am7

77
G
D 9
G
G♯°
81
A m7
D 7
D 9
G
3
85
C 7
D♭7
C 7
F 7
E♭m6
F 7
89
B♭7
B 7
B♭7
E♭7
D 7
D 9
93
G
D 9
G
G♯°
97
A m7
D 7
D 9
G
2

B♭ CLARINET

ROSE ROOM

Harry Williams and Art Hickman

Moderately bright

29 E♭m B♭ G7 B♭ F♯7
33 C9 F7 B♭ B♭7 B♭° E♭m B♭ F♯7
37 C9 F7 B♭Maj9 B♭6
41 B♭7 E♭Maj9 E♭6
45 E♭m B♭ G7
49 C7 F7 C7(♭5) F7 B♭
53 C9 F7 B♭Maj9 B♭6
57 B♭7 E♭Maj9 E♭6
61 E♭m B♭ G7 B♭
65 C9 F7 B♭ B♭7 B♭° E♭m B♭ F♯7

C 9
F 7
B♭Maj9
B♭6
B♭7
E♭Maj9
E♭6
E♭m
B♭
G 7
C 7
F 7
C 7(♭5)
F 7
B♭
C 9
F 7
B♭Maj9
B♭6
B♭7
E♭Maj9
E♭6
D.S. al CODA
CODA
B♭
2

This page intentionally left blank to facilitate page turns.

B♭ CLARINET

WHAT CAN I SAY AFTER I SAY I'M SORRY?

WHAT CAN I SAY AFTER I SAY I'M SORRY?
Walter Donaldson and Abe Lyman

CLAR. SOLO
37 G GMaj7 G7 C
41 Cm6 D7 G
45 GMaj7 G6 B♭° Am B B♭ Am
49 D7 Am7 D7 D7 Am7 D7 G G° D7 G E° D7
53 G GMaj7 G7 C
3
57 Cm6 D7 G
3 3
61 Dm6 E7 Dm6 E7 Am
65 Am7 D7 G
3
69 G GMaj7 G7 C
73 Cm6 G
77 GMaj7 G6 B♭° Am B B♭ Am
81 D7 Am7 D7 D7 Am7 D7 G G° D7 G E° D7

85
G
GMaj7
G7
C
89
Cm6
D7
G
93
Dm6
E7
Dm6
E7
Am
97
Am7
D7
G
101
G
GMaj7
G7
C
105
Cm6
D7
G
3
3
109
GMaj7
G6
B♭°
Am
B
B♭
Am
113
D7
Am7
D7
D7
Am7
D7
G
G°
D7
G
E°
D7
117
G
GMaj7
G7
C
121
Cm6
D7
G
125
Dm6
E7
Dm6
E7
Am
129
Am7
D7
G

MORE GREAT CLARINET PUBLICATIONS FROM

Music Minus One

CLASSICAL PUBLICATIONS

Advanced Contest Solos for Clarinet, Volume 1

Brahms • Hindemith • Mozart
Performed by Stanley Drucker
Accompaniment: Judith Olson, piano
Book/Online Audio
00400630 .... $14.99

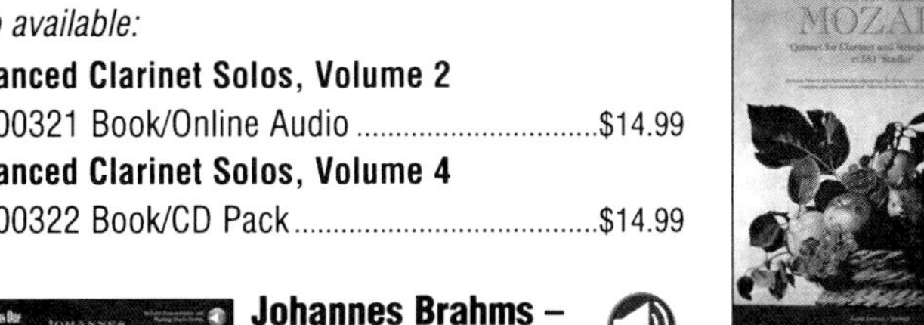

Also available:
Advanced Clarinet Solos, Volume 2
00400321 Book/Online Audio $14.99
Advanced Clarinet Solos, Volume 4
00400322 Book/CD Pack $14.99

Johannes Brahms – Clarinet Quintet in B Minor, Op. 115
Performed by Collete Galante
Accompaniment: The Classic String Quartet
Book/Online Audio
00400323 .... $19.99

Johannes Brahms – Sonatas for Clarinet and Piano, Op. 120
No. 1 in F Minor & No. 2 in E-Flat Minor
Performed by Jerome Bunke
Accompaniment: Hidemitsu Hayashi, piano
Book/2-CD Set
00400046 .... $19.99

The Clarinetist
Classical Pieces for Clarinet and Piano
Performed by Anton Hollich
Accompaniment: Harriet Wingreen, piano
Book/2-CD Set
00400122 .... $14.99

Clarinet Solos
Weber – Concertino, Op. 26 & Beethoven – Trio No. 4, Op. 11
Performed by Keith Dwyer
Accompaniment: The Stuttgart Festival Orchestra
Book/Online Audio
00400605 .... $19.99

W.A. Mozart – Clarinet Concerto in A Major, KV 622
Performed by Denitza Lavchieva
Accompaniment: Tempi Concertati Chamber Orchestra
Book/Online Audio
00400047 .... $19.99

W.A. Mozart – Quintet for Clarinet and Strings in A Major, KV581 "Stadler"
Performed by Keith Dwyer
Accompaniment: The Cassini Ensemble
Book/Online Audio
00400314 .... $19.99

Robert Schumann – Fantasy Pieces, Op. 73 & Three Romances, Op. 94
Performed by Jerome Bunke
Accompaniment: Hidemitsu Hayashi, piano
Book/Online Audio
00400316 .... $14.99

Carl Maria von Weber – Clarinet Concerto No. 1 F Minor, Op. 73 & Carl Stamitz – Concerto No. 3 in B-Flat Major
Performed by Keith Dwyer
Accompaniment: Stuttgart Festival Orchestra
Book/Online Audio
00400586 .... $19.99

POP/STANDARDS

Play the Music of Burt Bacharach
Performed by Tim Gordon
Accompaniment: The Jack Six All-Star Orchestra
Book/CD Pack
00400636 .... $14.99

Sinatra Set to Music
Performed by Ron Odrich
Accompaniment: The Al Raymond Orchestra
Book/Online Audio
00400711 .... $14.99

JAZZ/SWING

From Dixie to Swing
For Clarinet & Soprano Sax
Performed by Kenny Davern
Accompaniment: The Dick Wellstood All-Stars
Book/Online Audio
00400613 .... $14.99

New Orleans Classics
Performed by Tim Laughlin
Accompaniment: Tim Laughlin's New Orleans All Stars
Book/Online Audio
00400024 .... $19.99

Swing with a Band
Performed by Tim Gordon
Book/Online Audio
00400637 .... $14.99

What Is This Thing Called Jazz?
A Jazz Man's Approach to Great Standards
Performed by Ron Odrich
Book/CD Pack
00400681 .... $14.99

To see a full listing of Music Minus One publications, visit
halleonard.com/MusicMinusOne

Prices, contents, and availability subject to change without notice.